Ten SECRETS
You Must Know
Before Hiring
A LAWYER

Ten SECRETS
You Must Know
Before Hiring
A LAWYER

Joan E. Farr

Ten SECRETS You Must Know Before Hiring a Lawyer

Printed in the United States of America

Library of Congress Control Number: 2003106858

ISBN: 0-9744618-0-6

Published by Association for Honest Attorneys
              P.O. Box 558
              Derby KS 67037

Illustrations, cover and page design by Bear Hollow Art Works

To order online: www.assocforhonestattys.com

"Discourage litigation. Persuade your neighbors to compromise whenever you can. Point out to them the nominal winner is often a real loser in fees, expenses and waste of time."

A. Lincoln

＊

To Jeff
for encouraging me

To Abe
for inspiring me

To Mark
for loving me

＊

Contents

Preface

You may be wondering what a 47-year-old mother of four with no law degree could possibly know about the inner workings of our legal system. Well, it's a long story. They say experience is the best teacher, and that would have to be the main source of my knowledge.

I first became interested in the area of law when I graduated from high school. I had grown up learning about some of the legal battles my widowed mother had fought on her own. But having watched her sit at a typewriter for so many years as a court reporter and legal secretary, I decided that such a boring desk job was not for me. As a result, I started junior college in 1973 with a major in Police Science since it was my desire to become a police officer. This was a profession, I believed, involving excitement and action to the max. Friends teased me about wanting to become a "Charlie's Angel," but I had begun pursuing my career goals long before that TV program went on the air.

My major changed several times, but I finally received a Bachelor of Science degree in Administration of Justice from Wichita State University in 1977. I then received my Master's Degree in 1981 and had written my thesis on "The Evolvement and Acceptance of Women as Police Officers." I would have gone on to law school in Topeka or at the University of Kansas at that point; but unfortunately, I was madly in love with someone and didn't want to leave town. Yes, that was one of my bigger mistakes, for the guy eventually went off and married someone else.

Following my heartbreak, I got a taste of life on the police force when I became a traffic investigator for the City of Wichita from 1982 to 1984. Some of my legal experience is derived from having to testify in civil litigation involving traffic accidents during that time. The rest has come from observing the legal system for over 25 years, hearing about legal battles others had encountered, and from my own experiences in three lawsuits: a paternity suit (1987), breach of contract (1988), and a custody battle (1989). These were enough to convince me that I wanted to avoid any future lawsuits if at all possible.

Still, most of my background for understanding the legal system comes from a flood property damage lawsuit in 2000 and the astounding chain of events that ensued. That is, I am a general building contractor and was the first female builder to join the Wichita Area Builders' Association in 1999. The lawsuit involved construction of my first home in the building business and involved negligence claims which later evolved into conspiracy and fraud by the defendants and their attorneys. They influenced our previous attorney to persuade us we had no case, induced other attorneys not to represent us, and provoked the news media not to do a story so we couldn't get an attorney. I was forced to file the suit myself in March, 2001 and have been acting as my own attorney since that time. In more than two years of *pro se* litigation, I have consulted over 60 attorneys for advice on our case. Between April and December 2001, this involved some 26 hearings against nine defendants represented by six corporate attorneys. My health suffered severely, and the defendants ignored numerous requests to settle. Sedgwick County District Court in Wichita, Kansas dismissed our claims in December 2001, and we filed an appeal.

On July 3, 2003 the Kansas Court of Appeals affirmed the lower court's decision. The matter is currently awaiting a decision by the Kansas Supreme Court. I believe that, if the Constitution guarantees our right to be represented by an attorney in a criminal matter, we should have that right in a civil matter as well. Since it is my ardent belief that our Fifth Amendment right to due process of law was violated (they persuaded other attorneys not to represent us), it is my hope to reach the United States Supreme Court with the issues presented, if necessary. All this has led to my belief that: (1) no matter how good your case is, the side with the most money to pay their attorney wins, and (2) attorneys are "beating people up" (emotionally) to win lawsuits and getting away with it. In general, if the judicial system is all about money, shouldn't it be all about justice? I am hoping there will be some justice by the time this is all over.

I have written this book to help

people. Frequently, we can fear something simply because we don't understand it. So it is with the legal system for most people. My experience has shown me that many good lawyers do exist—because I could never have gotten this far without them—but too many of them use illegal and unethical means to win their cases. They "break the law to make the law," so to speak. Lawyers have long been criticized and made the butt of numerous jokes, but many Americans don't know *exactly* what makes them so despicable. The trade secrets of the legal profession contained in this book will give you a better understanding of these realities.

As many authors do, I have chosen to use my maiden name as my pen name—for reasons of heritage as well as privacy. It was also my husband's wish. This book is a compilation of my theories and opinions based on my experiences. It is meant for rich people, poor people, struggling people, all people. In sharing, I hope that the knowledge of the legal events in my life will help you save your hard-earned money and reduce your stress by avoiding lawsuits and keeping lawyers from taking advantage of you. Ultimately, it is my wish that unethical attorneys will no longer be allowed to use intentional emotional distress and other illegal means to win their cases. It is up to each of us to make sure this stops happening.

⌒⌒⌒ The Story ⌒⌒⌒

It all started in June, 1999 when I decided to leave my job at Boeing after 17 years to design, build and decorate spec homes for resale. After completing my first home in October, 1999, I received much publicity when the newspaper wrote a front page article about me as the first female Builder to join the Wichita Area Builders' Association ("Wife, Mother, General Contractor, . . . " *The*

Wichita Eagle, Oct. 2, 1999, p. 1.) The president of our local homebuilders' association (HBA) had been friendly toward me, even commenting to me once at a home show: "Stick with me, and I'll make you a star." At the time, I wasn't quite sure what he meant. Things were going well, I thought, until another builder constructed a home next to mine. He built on a natural flow of drainage hidden by trees, causing the backyard of my property to flood (an area 150 ft. long, 25 ft. wide, and up to 2 ft. deep). The water sat for months, became home to a family of ducks, and caused us to lose several contracts and numerous potential buyers. Our local HBA president became involved and advised me to just add fill dirt; however, inspectors disagreed, telling me that in a 6-10 inch rain, the home would likely flood. As it turned out, the developer and the survey company had failed to include a necessary drainage easement off the back of the lots. We were struggling financially in my new career, and my husband was turned down for a $4000 signature loan to buy fill dirt as a temporary solution. Inspectors informed me that the proper "fix" was to install a drain in the ground and excavate under the road into an area pond. This would achieve proper drainage for my lot as well as four other lots; however, the cost was anywhere from $60,000 to $100,000. The responsible parties refused to do anything. Although they were well aware of our financial difficulties, the solution offered by our local HBA president was to repair the flooding at our own expense; and if the matter went to court, I would be ruined as a builder. When I threatened publicity, I believe the vendetta began.

In April, 2000, I hired an attorney who was a family friend (or so I thought) to represent us on a contingency basis. He reviewed the facts and confidently prepared a negligence petition against the builder, the developer, and the survey company. He later told me he was suing for a million dollars in damages, hoping to get us enough money to retire. A week later, however, he mysteriously dropped to $5,000 after discussing the matter with the opposing attorneys. For the next seven months, he refused to file the suit and tried to convince me that the three defendants had no responsibility for repair, they had big money and power, and that we couldn't win because we had neither one. During this time, my 17-year old son left home to live with relatives, telling me he thought it would be "easier for us to take care of three kids, instead of four." My mother had been dying of cancer at her home, and the stress I was under forced me to turn over executor duties to my brother. Because the house would not sell, we tried for seven months to manage the mortgages and bills for two homes, with 94% of my husband's monthly income going toward bills. I stayed on unemployment and looked for other work, cashed in an IRA and all our savings bonds, lived off of borrowed money from in-laws, and charged groceries until our credit cards were maxed out. I passed the real estate exam in July, 2000, hoping for an alternate career; but no one would hire me. I was deemed "Typhoid Mary" because of the impending litigation and was forced to let my real estate license expire.

I contacted our local HBA president in July, 2000 as to whether I could sell the home I'd built in good faith, knowing there might be a future flooding problem. He assured me that I did not have to disclose a problem that I didn't know for sure would occur. Toward the end of the conversation, he commented: "You won't make those mistakes again, will you?" In August, 2000, I underwent skin cancer surgery in Kansas City, the severity of which my family physician agreed was due to stress. Our bank turned down my request to accept the deed in lieu of foreclosure on the house we had built, and I received no response from a letter I sent to our local HBA president asking for his help in locating an investor to buy it. My husband and I had entered counseling at our church and were nearing bankruptcy when my mother's death benefits paid $6000 in early September, 2000. We used the money to buy fill dirt and sold the home the following week, praying that the flooding would not continue.

In October, 2000, our attorney told me that he had negotiated a settlement offer of $10,000 and suggested we take it because, as he insisted, the defendants didn't have to give us anything, nor did they have to repair the flooding problem (even though I later learned there were numerous statutes, ordinances, and laws they had violated in this regard.)

My husband and I were near a divorce over the whole situation. That is, he continued to believe that everything our attorney was telling us was true simply because he was an attorney while I continued to be skeptical and unsure. But in order to prevent my marriage from breaking up, I signed the settlement agreement and returned it. Our lawyer then sent it back, telling me that the defendants wanted me to sign that the people who bought the house would not sue them either, and he had changed the settlement amount to "one dollar, and other valuable consideration." It was at that moment that I realized something was going on, and I was finally able to convince my husband that we needed to disengage his services—which we did immediately.

The next day, I received a routine phone call from an insurance company, telling me that I could file an insurance claim against the builder in this matter. The agent wondered why my attorney had not told me this. Although I pursued it all the way to the Kansas Insurance Commission, they advised us that the courts would have to decide the matter.

In December, 2000, I learned that in addition to flooding from the drainage of the adjacent subdivision, a possible wetlands area existed on the back of the property I had built on, also hidden by trees. A third inspector also agreed that the home that I had built would flood in a 6-10 inch rain. In March, 2001, I decided to file the lawsuit myself, hoping that the news media would do a story and an attorney would take our case. The backyard of the property flooded again after only two inches of rain, and the homeowners told me they were afraid. After numerous contacts with the local media, however, I became convinced that even they had been influenced not to do a story. Although I had been in constant e-mail contact with the Wichita reporter who wrote the original story about me, he admitted that politics existed, even in newspaper writing. Likewise, I received no help from the Sedgwick County District Attorney's office in regard to consumer fraud, the Kansas State Board of Technical Professions, or the Kansas Securities Commission after learning that the developer appeared to be in violation of the Kansas Uniform Land Sales Practices Act (he had misrepresented the properties and failed to give us any drainage information prior to purchase).

Meanwhile, I also contacted state representatives, the Kansas Attorney General's Office, the National Association of Homebuilders, the NAHB Women's Council, the American Civil Liberties Union (ACLU), and the National Organization for Women (NOW). It was apparent to me that the defendants and their attorneys were persuading other attorneys and agencies not to represent us so we would lose our case. In a phone conversation with our local HBA president in May 2001, he had demanded to know the name of one attorney who was assisting me and vowed to find out who he was. Shortly afterward, I never heard from this attorney again. Another lawyer even admitted to me in front of witnesses in June, 2001, "They're just going to keep beating you up until they wear you down." The county inspector I had befriended thought that with emotions rising my life might be in danger. He cautioned me to "just be careful while you're driving." When he later signed an affidavit to this effect, our HBA president threatened to have him fired or sue him for defamation if he did not change his statement. During this time, my 13-year old son ran away and was rumored to be suicidal. When we found him and brought him home, he was very distraught over our financial situation, and told me: "I just don't want to have to worry (about money) any more."

My health continued to suffer while I tried to handle the lawsuit on my own against six corporate attorneys. I was trying to figure out how to litigate, having to actually litigate, and attempting to find an attorney for a period of nine months. As we went through some 26 hearings, I typed my own court briefs and letters, made copies at a print shop, drove to Wichita to file them at the courthouse, and mailed them to all of the parties in time to meet deadlines. I received assistance over the phone from over 45 attorneys, many of whom helped me until they had discussions with opposing attorneys. Then I would never hear from them again. I contacted 18 drainage experts to obtain a report needed by the Court, but many declined for fear their business would be influenced. Fortunately, I managed to acquire the help of a drainage expert in Oklahoma City and one in Lawrence, Kansas. In August, 2001, the Court found that my supporting expert witness reports "were impressive" and allowed me to add claims of civil conspiracy, collusion, and fraud against the defendants. This included my former attorney and the local HBA president. I implicated the opposing attorneys for assisting their clients and even uncovered a letter from one of the attorneys to his client that clearly showed the conspiracy took place. As we had neared to settling for $10,000 the year before, the builder's attorney was instructing his client to issue a check from his own business "so that I would not know that insurance was involved." It went on to state that they were afraid that "if [I] found out insurance was involved, it would blow the whole settlement." Although this was the smoking gun to support our claims of fraud and conspiracy, the district court would not allow the letter as evidence, telling me it was likely "attorney-client privileged." From that point on, it seemed the Court found reason to rule in favor of the defendants. Although I had made numerous attempts to try to settle the matter, they were ignored by defense counsel. I believe that in some cases, they never even told their clients so that the matter would drag on and they would make more money. One attorney sent me harassing letters to demand dismissal of his client, threatening to sue us for malicious prosecution and thousands in attorney fees as well as taking our non-exempt property and garnishing my husband's wages. Three weeks later, while trying to conduct nine depositions and meet deadlines in the lawsuit, I collapsed from an anxiety attack and was in bed for two days. Even though clear and convincing evidence had been presented and altogether seven experts (including the original engineer) stated that there should have been a drainage easement across the back of the lots, my hopes for a jury trial were dashed on December 21, 2001. The District Court dismissed my claims against all the defendants because I did not follow a Supreme Court rule in preparing my paperwork.

In January 2002, I began to do research to file an appeal in our case and noticed that much of the evidence in my court file was missing. Only attorneys are allowed to check out court files, and the "smoking gun" letter had even been detached from my court brief. I also found that depositions and even court transcripts had been altered. Such discrepancies were noted in our appellate court brief and the reply brief later filed with the Kansas Court of Appeals. During this time, I was expelled from our local HBA association for filing "false litigation." I had been labeled "Typhoid Mary" and "Sue-crazy" by the building and real estate industry, and even close friends would no longer associate with us. My construction business suffered to the point that we were only able to build three houses between 1999 and 2003. Although my homes were uniquely designed, built and decorated, they were difficult to sell because stories had spread and realtors would steer clear. I held my own open houses, but signs were stolen on several occasions and efforts were made to hold up my closings. After four years of business, I was never able to draw a salary as president of my construction company.

In March, 2002, I felt the need to let other people know about the issues I had discovered and wrote an editorial called "Legal Abuse: Has It Happened to You?" I sent it to 100 major newspapers across the country, including our local area, but it was printed by no one. I wrote to *USA Today, Newsweek, Time, People,* CBS, ABC, NBC, CNN, ESPN, and Oprah—but with no response. I felt like their legal departments had taken one look and canned it. I also believed from comments made in our local HBA newsletter that a national plan had been put in place to quash any publicity by our local president who admitted during his deposition that he had contacts in Washington.

In July 2002, several months after filing our appeal and the discovery of evidence tampering, our local police and the district attorney's office brought charges against my 14-year old son for a school incident that had happened six months earlier. In January, 2002, my son had come home from school and confided that he did not want to attend the next day because he'd heard that someone was going to shoot up the school at the afternoon assembly. Realizing that he wasn't joking, I contacted our local (small town) police department and made a report. Several hours later, the police decided my son had made up the story. He was arrested, fingerprinted, had a mug shot taken, was handcuffed and booked into the juvenile detention center in nearby Wichita. This was devastating since he had no prior police record.

When I came to pick him up later that night, the intake officer told me in a hushed voice, "I don't want to say that an officer made a mistake, but I have seen where officers make mistakes." She said she believed my son was telling the truth, that he was trying to protect a boy he thought would commit suicide if questioned. The intake officer told me she was going to call the local police department right away and give them the information. My son was then released to my custody.

Interestingly enough, I later discovered that the police had ransacked the boy's home later that night, and he was arrested at school the next day. Yet in July, 2002—*six months after the incident* and after I had noticed missing and altered court documents in my lawsuit—charges were brought by the local police and the district attorney's office against my son for Filing a False Alarm. *This made no sense because I, myself, had made the call to the police.* But I had commented before the court at an earlier hearing in my lawsuit that "grownups can have their issues, but you don't hurt the children." At that point, the defense attorneys knew that my children were my weakness, that I was most vulnerable where their safety and wellbeing are concerned. I believe they resorted to having our local police department and district attorney's office file baseless charges against my son to cause us further intentional emotional distress. An out-of-area attorney told me that such ridiculous charges should just be dismissed, but both an attorney we hired and two court-appointed attorneys refused to pursue this request. I wrote to the county commissioner, the district attorney, attorney general, and at the suggestion of Columbine High School, even the governor of Kansas. All of them responded that they could offer no assistance because it was a legal matter. I felt that these circumstances were just too *weird* to be simply the normal run of events.

My son continued for months in therapy, was put on depression medication, and—since he had ruined his clean record—felt like he was destined for a life of crime. I think the only thing that got him through the whole ordeal was explaining to him how misguided I think our legal system is and that I am fighting to make sure the unethical practices of attorneys do not continue.

And the outcome for my son? A year after the police brought their trumped up charges, we finally went before the judge. The day before his trial, an attorney friend had pointed out to me that they'd had six months to bring my son to trial. Since it had been a whole year, his Sixth Amendment right to a speedy trial had been violated, and *that was reason to dismiss the charges.* Our court-appointed attorney still refused. Then I looked up the statute online and learned that he had been incorrectly charged with filing a false *fire* alarm! The case was still tried before a judge. Despite the fact that two other boys testified they'd heard the alleged shooter say he was going to shoot up the school, the judge hammered my son for his actions. Before finally dismissing the charges, he even looked for something else to charge him with.

I strongly believed that the allegations against my son were prompted by the defendants and their counsel. I had written to President Bush twice in 2002 regarding the lack of justice in our justice system and had sent him my editorial. I was surprised when he wrote back in November 2002 to thank me for my concern about "corporate fraud."

Oral arguments in our lawsuit were heard by the Kansas Court of Appeals on April 23, 2003 in which I addressed the two main issues in our case: (1) that no matter how good your case is, the side with the most money to pay their attorney wins; and (2) that attorneys should not be allowed to beat people up to win lawsuits. That same day, I filed a second lawsuit naming the defendants, the attorneys, and the insurance companies involved—some sixteen defendants—to be combined with the first lawsuit eventually. The local president managed to get himself dismissed shortly thereafter, and the rest of the defendants jumped on the bandwagon to do the same. The opposing attorneys threatened to have me pay their fees and court costs; so in May, I was legally advised to file a voluntary dismissal of the second suit with possible re-filing after six months, pending the appellate court's decision. Luckily, this was granted by the district court.

My desire was to pursue our case

to the United States Supreme Court, if necessary, hoping for justice and a published opinion that would reveal to people the realities of our legal system. But in case this never happens, I have written this book. In April, 2003, I also founded the Association for Honest Attorneys ("A.H.A!")—a non-profit organization dedicated to discouraging civil litigation, creating public awareness of the illegal and unethical practices of many attorneys, and seeking "justice for *all*."

Although this book is mainly concerned with civil litigation, I believe the following ten secrets are what you must know before hiring a lawyer for *any* reason.

Chapter One:
Three Reasons
An Attorney
Takes A Case

1. What are your claims?
2. Can you prove them?
3. Collectability

An attorney actually told me in August of 2001 that these are uppermost in the minds of the legal profession when members of it accept a case. An attorney can advise you on what your claims are (that is, the legal ways in which you have been harmed such as negligence, breach of contract, fraud, etc.) and whether you have adequate evidence to support them (witnesses, contracts, documents, etc.). These are pretty straightforward and self-explanatory. The idea of collectability, however, might benefit from some further discussion. This concept refers to the chances of winning and collecting from the other side as well as the ability of the client to pay attorney fees even if he or she doesn't win the case.

Normally an attorney will take your case whether it is strong or not on the premise that you pay him a retainer. But please note: ***never*** agree to this without knowing what his hourly charge is and having him document that he will refund any unused portion of your money. When the funds run out, he will expect you to continue paying him monthly.

If he accepts your case on a contingency, he is doing so because your case appears strong, the outcome looks favorable to your winning, and he will be able to collect in the end. On the other hand, you can generally expect that, if your case is not solid and you don't have much money, your chances of adequate representation are lessened. Your chances of winning are nil.

Keep this important reality in mind: when you hire an attorney, it is doubtful he is really working for you. According to my personal observations, he is operating in conjunction with the opposing attorney to decide what the outcome will be and who should win. Certainly we want to believe that the result is based on the evidence provided by both sides; but from what I have seen, it actually depends on which attorney is getting paid the most money by his client. What many people don't realize is that there are many different points of law on which a case can be won or lost, and they all seem very rational and believable. If you pay your attorney more than the opposing side is paying theirs, he will find you the point of law to win your case. From my experiences in the legal system, I have sadly concluded that a lack of justice exists because, no matter how good your case is, the side with the most money (to pay their attorney) wins.

So the question remains: if the majority of attorneys are loyal to money rather than what is right and true, does justice really exist in our society today? Apparently not.

Justice

Chapter Two:
It's All A Game

You may recall this scene from the movie "Erin Brockovich." With fanfare the opposing attorneys are escorted into the conference room, puffing out their most intimidating chests; and attorney Ed Masry says under his breath to Erin, "Let the games begin. . . ."

The sooner you realize that these individuals are just playing a game—one of intimidation—the better off you'll be. They will use any number of tactics to try to persuade you one way or another;

a notable, highly effective one of these is intentional emotional distress. In my own negligence/fraud lawsuit, for example, they tried threatening us, harassing us, and finally resorted to cheating to win the case. What sort of cheating, you wonder? When I decided to appeal our lawsuit, I noticed that numerous exhibits were missing from the court file when only attorneys are allowed to check this out; and a key exhibit had been detached from a court document so it would appear I had made a mistake. I also noticed there were numerous alterations to court transcripts and depositions. One of my drainage experts had made the statement that the builder "had to know he was going to cause me a problem—it doesn't take a rocket scientist to figure that out." This statement was missing entirely from his deposition. The developer admitted to me in his deposition that he was a millionaire, but this was also missing. At the final hearing where all of the defendants were dismissed, the judge confessed he had worked at the law firm of the developer five years earlier, and I objected by saying, "We don't think you should hear this case." This statement was nowhere to be found in the court transcript.

The insurance companies also seem engaged in the game. It was the legal duty of my previous attorney to tell us that the defendants had liability insurance to cover the flooding they had caused. But he never did. It was in November 2000 that he had urged me to settle for $10,000 (rather than the $1,000,000 he had suggested initially) with no offer by the defendants to repair the continuing flooding problem. He had persuaded me that this was all I was going to get, that they didn't have to give me anything, and to immediately sign the settlement agreement. The stress over the matter was all but destroying my marriage which is why I put my name on the line.

But as I mentioned, he sent it back,

announcing that the other side wanted revisions. One of these was for me to sign for the people to whom I had sold the property that they wouldn't sue them either. This is when I also noticed that the amount had changed from $10,000 to "$1.00, and other valuable consideration." Naturally, I asked why the number had been modified, and he snapped: "Oh, just sign it anyway—we all know it's $10,000!" Without delay, I withdrew my acceptance and terminated his services, finally able to convince my husband that our "family friend" attorney had not been working for us.

The helpful insurance agent who had phoned me and advised that liability insurance covered such matters also suggested that I make a list of our damages, then call around to find out what company the builder was using. When I did this and discovered who the builder's insurance company was, they ignored my list and went along with the $10,000 offered by the attorneys. The obliging insurance representative had also advised me to write to the state insurance commissioner, who acted as judge and jury in such concerns. Unfortunately, the defendants' influence was far-reaching because their response two months later stated that the courts would have to decide the matter. This led to my belief that the attorneys and insurance companies worked closely together.

It was in November 2000 that the three defendants (the builder, developer, and survey company) were asked by their counsel to "ante up" $3300 each when the settlement was about to go through for $10,000. After I had filed the lawsuit, I tried to acquire a waiver of the attorney-client privilege, but it was denied. During discovery, I had tried desperately to obtain any information I could between the defendants and their insurance companies. All of the defense attorneys claimed their clients' insurance files were indeed "attorney-client privileged"; but amazingly enough, one of the attorneys confided to me that this really wasn't true. In fact, he went so far as to allow me a look in his client's insurance file. Prior to this, of course, he had redacted (removed) any documents that he thought would incriminate his client; at least this was his intention.

When I sat in the darkened room reviewing the defendant's insurance file, I found a letter from his previous attorney to him. Obviously his new attorney— the one giving me access to these documents—had failed to snatch it out of my view before he gave me the folder. The letter indicated that *the insurance company* had sent the settlement check for $3300 but that he wanted his client to issue a check from his own office so that I "would not know that insurance was involved." It went on to state: "I think (rightly so) they are concerned that if she knows there is insurance the settlement may fall apart." I almost jumped out of my skin when I stumbled across this admission since it clearly supported my claims of civil conspiracy and fraud. I was elated in thinking that justice might actually prevail.

Unfortunately, the judge at a subsequent hearing ruled that the letter I had found was probably "attorney-client privileged." After he left the room, I disgustedly sat there with the opposing attorneys and muttered, "Guess you got out of that one." Smirking happily, one replied, "That's the name of the game!"

I am left wondering about the laws forbidding people from providing false information to insurance companies so they will not be defrauded. Where are the laws to punish insurance companies for inadequate settlements or falsely settling claims? In our case, it was not only the defendants but the insurance companies as well who committed fraud against us.

Chapter Three: Don't Believe Everything An Attorney Tells You

You might be offered pearls like these:

- You can't win; you have no money.
- No one else will represent you.
- You'll lose—they have big power and
    money.
- They don't have to give you anything.
- You need an affidavit from someone else
    (who agrees with what you say), or you

are going to lose at the hearing.

▭ There is no crusade here; your right to due process hasn't been violated.

▭ You only have a $5000 to $10,000 case

▭ Your damages are not what you think they are.

I heard all of these comments during my lawsuit from attorneys and, in some cases, the judges themselves. The opposition kept trying to persuade me that my claims were only worth $10,000 at best; even one of the judges tried to win me over to this point of view during one of the hearings. But in fact, I found these comments altogether untrue once I had researched case law regarding my claims.

Our previous attorney's initial assurance that, by golly, we had a million dollar lawsuit on the table, a grand amount he deflated a week later to a mere

$5,000, should be evidence enough to demonstrate how an attorney's comments cannot always be trusted. Because I was later directed to file an ethics complaint against this man, one attorney confided to me that the defense attorneys' strategy would be to manipulate my case so it would either result in the original settlement amount or be dismissed. In this way, our former attorney would cunningly be absolved from his wrongdoing against us. Our society holds the legal profession in such very high esteem—as if attorneys are God's assistants and their words are spoken in His behalf. But trust me—their exalted view has little to do with truth in too many cases.

In August 2001, I managed to find another attorney I thought would represent us. I paid him $1500, but his services were short-lived. He backed out just before a hearing from fear of sanctions by the court if we lost. (The court can "sanction" you—order you to pay attorney fees and/or other court costs—if they find that you filed an unnecessary motion for a hearing without good reason.) Although this attorney seemed supportive and enthusiastic at first, he eventually fell under their grasp. When I heard him say, "There's no crusade here. Your right to due process of law was not violated," I knew immediately that it was all over with him, too. In many cases, attorneys are convinced by opposing attorneys to persuade their clients in a certain manner and, in exchange, are promised more business. I found it interesting several months later when I ran into another attorney I had known from college classes long ago. As we chatted, I happened to mention that they had kept me from getting an attorney to represent us. "Yep," he said, "they violated your right to due process of law."

In other words, if you feel skeptical of what you're hearing from your lawyer, seek another opinion. It should be clear that your representation by such counsel would be lacking, especially if you have researched similar cases and determined that your claims are valid and well supported.

For most attorneys, an initial consultation is free. Many of them will chat with you over the phone at no charge to discuss your situation and whether they would be willing to handle it. Most attorneys specialize in one area or another, and this is usually indicated in the yellow pages of your phone book. If you have time, get two or three opinions just as you would with a medical condition. Even still, judging from what I've learned, keep in mind that no matter how good your case may be, the side with the most money (to pay their attorney) wins. If you are the plaintiff and the defendant(s) have more money to throw at their counsel, you are better off not to file suit, particularly if your damages are minor. Hard as this may be to hear, it is best to save your money and chalk it up to valuable lessons learned.

Altogether, the monetary expenses

we incurred from trying to litigate ourselves (legal advice, court costs, depositions, etc.) totaled about $20,000 in a two-year period. If your adversary(s) are not as thoroughly obstinant as ours, you'd be surprised how much of your time and money could be saved by saying, "I'm sorry for what's happened. Can we work this out?"

The toll on my health was much higher when I realized the effect of spending over 2000 hours of effort involved. I had tried continually to settle the matter both verbally and in correspondence with the defense attorneys, especially after 9/11. Yet I doubt that my efforts ever reached their clients since dragging out the case put more money in the attorneys' pockets. Later, I wrote letters to the defendants themselves in an attempt to settle. Everyone in the opposition was aware that my health was deteriorating from the stress the situation involved, but still the defendants listened to their counsel and ignored my attempts to deal with them directly. I can imagine the defense team advising their clients and each other as the suit went along: "Oh, she doesn't have any money—she'll drop it soon"; "We'll make sure no one represents her, then she'll drop the suit"; "She'll break sooner or later." When their predictions missed the mark and the litigation continued through 26 hearings, I can certainly guess that the defendants themselves were becoming irate over the mounting attorney fees either they or their insurance companies had to pay. Not surprisingly, their insurance rates must have risen significantly as a result. At that point, even they must have realized that you can't believe everything spewing from the mouth of one representing the legal profession.

You have no doubt noticed the numbers of frivolous, even ridiculous, lawsuits these days brought by individuals, some of whom were paid in the thousands, if not millions. Suing a fast food chain for becoming obese is one of the silliest examples of this trend. Clearly, attorneys are persuading people to sue large companies for such ludicrous incidents, tantalizing them with assurances of winning big bucks based upon their supposedly strong cases. It is my guess that most of these suits are based on a contingency fee where the attorney collects about 40% for winning. And why are we duped? Again, it's because we generally believe whatever judicial persons, pronouncing utterances from their lofty pedestals, tell us. After the grief and stress of litigation that they put you through, is it really worth it?

In general, then, the real winner in any lawsuit is the attorney who collects his excessive fees—whether the outcome is a victory or not. After all, he is just doing his job.

Chapter Four:
Your Attorney
Is Not Working
For You

During my lawsuit, a journalist shared this viewpoint with me: "How do you know your attorney is really working for you?" My immediate response was, "You don't!" because, in my opinion, he's not. You may have hired him, but his allegiance is not necessarily to you. As I noted previously, my observations have indicated that your attorney is deciding, together with opposing counsel (and even with the presiding judge), who should win your dispute. Again, you naturally believe the results of the case evolved from the evidence presented by both sides, but in reality they are based on which attorney is receiving the biggest bankroll from his client. All in all, if your opponent is determined to win no matter what the cost, do you really want to go there?

Let's consider an example from my experiences as a traffic investigator in the early 1980s. One day while I was waiting to testify in traffic court, an attorney approached me and asked if I would testify in a civil case the following day. He apologized for the short notice but assured me that my participation would not take long. Of course, I agreed. Upon my arrival the next morning, the attorney asking me the favor as well as the *opposing* attorney ushered me back into the judge's chambers before my testimony could be heard. The first lawyer announced what question he intended to ask me and wanted to know how I would answer. After telling him my response, he remarked: "Good. That's what we wanted you to say." I then queried, "Aren't you going to ask me this question, too?"—the other side of the coin, so to speak. "No," he replied, "because we want the jury to find 50 percent for the plaintiff and 50 percent for the defendant." Their intent was that if I never addressed the other half of the issue, they could get the result *they* were trying to achieve, regardless of who was at fault. I believe this instance further substantiates my point that no matter how good your case is, the side with the most money to pay their attorney comes out on top. In this particular situation, I believe both sides were paying their counsel equally.

Here is another example. Several years ago I received a jury summons and did my civic duty by showing up at the courthouse. The district attorney routinely asked me: "Is there any reason why you cannot be a juror in this case?" I could only be honest. Explaining that I had a master's degree in administration of justice, had worked for the police department for two years and testified in several cases, and had been involved in two lawsuits in the late 1980s, I confessed I had formed some strong opinions based on what I had seen through these experiences. Specifically, I told her that I knew attorneys ask some questions in court but *don't* ask others so they can manipulate the case in whatever direction they choose. As I told the judge, I didn't feel I could be on the jury because I was afraid I would be judging the guilt or innocence of a person based **not** on the evidence presented in court but on what I *thought* really happened. The district attorney was fuming, but the judge agreed that this was, indeed, a legitimate reason to excuse me from jury duty.

Be aware that your attorney and the opposing attorney are going to work together to discover the source of your weakness. In my case, they knew I had very little money. Cunningly, they will maneuver you into revealing your past history on whatever issue they find necessary to get you to give up your fight. Is there something from your past that you want to keep secret? Might there be something in your medical or employment records—which they *will* subpoena—that would tarnish your dignity or credibility? Is there something that would make you so distraught if it were revealed that you would crumble at the very thought? Realize that the attorneys, both yours and *theirs,* are always exchanging information about their clients so the outcome will be what they deem acceptable.

Again, it is my ardent belief that the results of the case will be based on who is paying his or her attorney the most money. Let me give you another personal illustration. In 1987, I dated a man for almost a year and became pregnant just as we were breaking up. We continued to stay friends until he bolted two weeks before our son was born, deciding that he must not be the father. Since I desperately needed child support, I was forced to file a paternity suit against him.

I vividly recall when both our attorneys insisted on our presence at the courthouse for a hearing. When we arrived, they proclaimed that the hearing had been cancelled and we should wait there in the hall while they discussed some important issues inside the courtroom. The attorneys were very well aware that this was an emotional time since my ex-boyfriend had walked out on us. Over two hours later, we were still camped in the hall as they conferred. Were they hoping we would argue and set the walls on fire so the case would drag out further, bringing them both more money? At one point, I went in to ask for a quarter for the parking meter, and the two of them fairly jumped out of their skins with startled reflexes and guilty expressions. I felt they had been trying to conceal their mere lounging in the room, doing nothing but stalling so they could make more money.

My attorney had mentioned to me that he and the opposing counsel really wanted to see our case go to trial. By now, my son's father and I were on speaking terms. As a single mother of two, it was quite a hardship to come up with the attorney fees in this matter. When I complained to the lawyer about my situation, he smiled and explained that the amount I was paying him was *nothing* compared to what the baby's father was having to fork over to his attorney! In that revealing moment, I realized I'd had enough of their games. I convinced my former boyfriend that the two were in cahoots with each other; and for once, he agreed. In spite of our situation, we fired both attorneys and were able to work out the matter ourselves.

I believe former Dallas attorney and judge Catherine Crier would agree with this philosophy. In her book *The Case Against Lawyers* she writes:

> Even former New York governor and once likely Supreme Court appointee Mario Cuomo succumbed to modern reality in a

2000 commencement address to young lawyers entitled "The Soul of the Profession." In describing the personal meaning of the practice of law, he focused not on the more noble aspects but instead on "putting food on the table . . . and getting the bills paid." He went on to say, "Billions of human beings have come and gone, and only an infinitesimal number of them have succeeded in making a difference in the development of this planet." So, why bother? Do your time and cash your checks. (Crier, Catherine. *The Case Against Lawyers.* New York: Broadway Books, 2002, p. 188.)

Justice

Chapter Five:
Attorneys
(Even Yours)
Are Trying
To Stress
You Out

If you've ever been involved in litigation, maybe you've lived through this scenario. Your attorney notifies you of a hearing. Your emotions get hyped up to the hilt. Sleep never comes the night before. You take off work. You dress for success. Your arrival at the courthouse is impeccably punctual. Upon entering the building, you are informed that the hearing has been postponed and, in fact, you didn't even need to be there in the first place. Should you conclude you're just having a bad day and were simply unlucky in the way things didn't come together this time? Probably not. This is a strategy concocted by both your attorney and theirs to *cause you stress* and ultimately achieve the end result *they* would like to achieve, namely that one of you will get fed up and call it quits.

Let me illustrate. I worked with a young woman in the mid-1980's who became pregnant and filed a paternity suit against the father. He was a promising young medical student, the pampered son of a wealthy family. They hired an attorney whose primary function was to use strategic methods of continually inflicting emotional stress on her in this manner for over a year and a half until the poor woman could take no more. All but predictably, she gave up without even acquiring child support for her son.

If intentional emotional distress is against the law, why are attorneys allowed to use it as a strategy to win lawsuits? These individuals are not above the law and certainly should not be allowed to "break the law to make the law." The problem lies with us, with our blind faith in their every word as informed truth. Supposing that, since they know the law, they will be in a hurry to tell us the truth about it, we put them on that proverbial pedestal and pay homage to their wisdom and clarity of thought with our cash. But instead of the truth, in many cases they will present one point of the law to us but not the other. From what I have researched and observed, for every case where a decision was rendered one way, there is another case that caused a verdict to be rendered yet another way.

For example, in my lawsuit I discovered there are at least two separate legal doctrines involving flooding. The defense attorneys argued that Kansas had long observed the "common enemy doctrine" in regard to flooding—the right to fend off surface water flowing onto one's property by adding fill dirt to keep the land from flooding. However, during my research at the law library, I discovered that the "natural flow doctrine" should apply which states that you cannot construct anything that will dam up the natural flow of a body of water such that it causes flooding to the property of another. In our case, the drainage from an adjacent subdivision was hidden by trees but had been flowing downhill onto our properties for ten years. Because the builder next to me constructed his home in the path of the stream *first* and later added a hundred loads of fill dirt to keep the water from flowing onto his house and property, it would seem obvious to any reasonable person that the "natural flow doctrine" should apply. (This was a contradiction to the ruling by the district court that the "common enemy doctrine" applied.) What many of us don't realize is that each case is different, and it comes down to what a reasonable and prudent person would believe—at least, this is the way it should be.

Naturally we suppose that justice does exist to some degree and that each case is fairly evaluated on its own set of circumstances. Yet again, money plays a significant role here; that is, your attorney will get a decision in your favor if you pay him more than the opposing attorney is getting. In fact, this manipulation can even carry over into a jury's functioning. I have seen instances where the lawyers ask only certain questions while avoiding others so the jury, with their purposely slanted view, will render a decision the way the counselors intend. As we have seen, this was true in the civil case where I testified as a police officer in the early '80s. The fact that O.J. Simpson was found not guilty should be another obvious indication.

Another strategy used by members of the legal profession is to do nothing. Typically, attorneys will not call you but wait for you to call them first. This starts the clock ticking for payment, and they can continue this a number of times if they so desire. This strategy drags your matter out further, causing you more stress and little satisfaction that anything is getting done. This tactic was used, for example, during my negligence/fraud lawsuit. I had already tried to work things out with the defendants when I hired our previous attorney *specifically* to file the suit. Instead, he did nothing but argue with me for seven months and try to persuade me that it shouldn't be filed.

Further, there were numerous ways that the defense attorneys tried to stress us out in that lawsuit. They sent harassing letters threatening to sue us for malicious prosecution, to garnish my husband's wages, and to have the sheriff seize all of our non-exempt property. Could they have gone forward with any of these menacing actions? It isn't likely because they knew we were in the right and because we had no money. As a matter of fact, quite early in our lawsuit I became aware that we were essentially "judgment proof"—we had nothing they could take from us financially. If you recall the three reasons an attorney accepts a case, specifically the third point, they knew they would not have been able to collect. In my view, understanding full well that we were broke, they went to plan B and tried to "beat us up," harass us—even so far as to severely traumatize my son by arresting him on baseless charges. When those strategies didn't work, they resorted to cheating to win (i.e. deleting documents from the court file, altering transcripts, etc.).

Chapter Six:
You Can
Represent
Yourself,
But Be Careful

In spite of everything, if you feel you must go forward with a lawsuit or otherwise represent yourself in a legal matter, there are a number of things you must know. First and foremost, it is a very time consuming matter. In order to determine whether your case is strong enough to proceed, you must do research and find other cases with similar circumstances to yours where the outcome is favorable from your point of view.

Where do you start with such research? Interestingly enough, statutes and laws are on the internet, but case law is not. In other words, you'll need to research your claims and similar case law at your local law library. You can pull similar cases on file at the clerk's office to prepare your pleadings prior to filing a petition. Call your state's legal service for any questions you may have. Keep in mind that, if your documents are not prepared accurately or if you fail to meet the necessary deadlines, the judge can dismiss your case on such technicalities. It's also a smart idea to send most of your documents registered and certified, requiring a returned receipt showing that the opposing attorney (or at least his office) received it. If you prefer, you can also hand-carry it to his or her office. Otherwise, he can say he never got it. This actually happened after one of our hearings. I had not understood the importance of using certified mail when sending a critical document requested by the judge to the opposing lawyers, and it was mysteriously "lost" in transit. Remember that it's all a game in the legal profession; don't take any chances.

How do you know what documents to file? You can look up cases similar to yours at the clerk's office since all lawsuits filed are a matter of public record. Ask them to make copies of petitions, answers, motions, etc. that attorneys have filed in other cases; then go by those documents (using your own words) to type up your own. Always ask for a jury trial in your paperwork (you have this Constitutional right) and you can change your mind later on, but your chances are better if you don't leave it up to one judge. If you need clarification about the meaning of a legal term or how to state something, call your state's legal services and they will let you talk to an attorney concerning any general questions for about $3.00 per minute. Don't forget to attach a certificate of service to your court document, or the judge is likely to throw your case out.

When you visit your local law library, what should you read? Your state's *Statues Annotated* along with the supplemental document ("supps," as they are called) will give you your state's laws in regard to civil suits as well as short blurbs of decisions in recent cases. You should become very familiar with this book, even read it cover to cover, if you're attempting the do-it-yourself method. *Black's Law Dictionary* is a must for looking up the meaning of legal terms you don't understand. *West's Digest* contains examples of cases decided according to your claims; you can look under subject headings such as Negligence, Fraud, Breach of Contract, etc. to find material appropriate to your situation. If you are filing a suit or an answer to a suit filed against you, you will need to quote whatever cases you find in your brief to support the arguments in your case. Your claims (also called "causes of action") can be looked up as well, so ask your law librarian where these and any other books may be found. Follow what you need to establish a prima facie case, literally "on its face," which means you are able to present enough evidence in your matter to win. If you don't have all of the evidence you need and don't think it will turn up during *discovery* (this is where both sides ask for and present evidence prior to trial), think twice about what you are doing. If you should lose your case, they can come back and file malicious prosecution claims against you but probably won't if you have little money and they can't collect. Always be aware of the time limits you have to prepare and file your documents as well as the *statute of limitations* (how much time you have to file your petition.) These are both found in your state's *Statutes Annotated.*

How much should you ask in damages? The petition our previous attorney was supposed to file asked for up to $75,000 for each claim we had. You will eventually have to itemize all of your losses, and there are several books at your law library that address the calculation of damages. I was not aware until later that you can ask for up to $250,000 for a claim of emotional distress, at least in Kansas (this varies from state to state). In addition, if you can prove your claim was intentional, that the opposition set out to hurt you on purpose, this amount could double or even triple if awarded by a jury.

What kind of evidence do you need? Pictures are like gold, one attorney told me. To prove our claims of negligence, we had pictures of the flooding in both 2000 and again in 2001, even an aerial photo which showed the long stream of water flowing from north to south and the home constructed by the builder clearly blocking its path. And though we had never been given any drainage information, we did discover a topographical drainage map which was so ambiguous that even our drainage experts said they couldn't understand it.

There are other kinds of evidence

as well, including your statement of what others will say in court (called *interrogatories),* any written documents or contracts, sworn statements which are notarized called *affidavits,* and of course, *depositions.* Taken before the trial, a deposition is a sworn statement transcribed by a court reporter in which the attorneys ask questions of a witness; this document may be used for trial later on. In our lawsuit, for example, the builder, developer, and engineer from the survey company all made statements that they had met together and decided to do nothing in regard to repairing the flooding they caused us (collusion). Both of our drainage experts submitted reports stating that there should have been a drainage easement and the house would flood in a heavy rain. The engineer himself admitted in his deposition that he should have put a drainage easement across the back of the lots! A county inspector confirmed that he had conversations with the builder as he began construction and stated in his affidavit that the builder "knew darn good and well" he was going to cause us a flooding problem but he was going to put the house there any-way—"he didn't care who got hurt." The letter from the attorney to the builder I mentioned earlier showed fraud on the part of the attorneys with their clients. But *in spite of such evidence,* our claims were still dismissed.

Don't let anyone fool you—this type of evidence is strong enough to show that your claims are justified. Furthermore, statements by someone else that a person acted to harm you intentionally can support a claim for *punitive damages—* an additional amount that you ask for as punishment and to keep that person from continuing his or her wrongdoing. In short, you should have enough evidence that a "reasonable person" will believe your claims are valid.

What happens after you file your lawsuit? The opposing attorney will file what is called an *answer* in regard to your petition of claims after which there will be a discovery hearing. Again *discovery* is a period of time in which each side tries to obtain evidence needed to prove or disprove the claims involved (affidavits, depositions, income tax returns, medical/employment records, etc.). Eventually, the other side may file what is called a Motion to Dismiss or a Motion for Summary Judgment. You need to file a response to any such motions, and this should be done within a specified time period. In Sedgwick County it was standard procedure to fax a response to the opposing attorney by 4:00 P.M. the day before and hand-carry a copy to the civil court presiding judge. It is probably different in every area, so it is best to call the court clerk's office to find out the proper procedure.

How should you conduct yourself at a hearing? There are several important things to remember. *Always be on time.* During my lawsuit, for instance, I had to appear at the docket call on Friday mornings at 9:00 A.M. at which time the civil court presiding judge would announce all of the cases for that day. When mine was read, I would stand and say: "That is for hearing, Your Honor." If you aren't there on time or fail to respond, the judge will usually grant in favor of the opposing attorney. In general, the civil court presiding judge will assign your hearing to one of the judges, and you immediately proceed to his courtroom. Once you have entered, *turn your cell phone off.* Always stand when the judge enters the room, and always stand when you speak. Address him as "Your Honor" or "Judge —," and although it happens on TV all the time, *never approach the bench.* Always stand behind the courtroom table or podium. Do not talk over the judge or the attorneys when they are speaking, or the judge will likely reprimand you when this happens. Listen carefully to whatever the judge says and comply with any requests; give him your utmost attention and respect. Regardless of what happens, *keep your cool.* When the hearing is over and the decision is rendered, always stand when the judge leaves the room.

There are many technicalities that the opposing attorneys can use to ask the court to dismiss your claims. For instance, I knew of a case while working for the police department where a wealthy man had been arrested for drunk driving, and his cherry red Mercedes Benz was towed away. The man appeared at trial with several attorneys; and even though the police officer's testimony against him and all of the evidence proved him guilty, his case was dismissed because it was never stated during the trial that his DUI occurred within Sedgwick County, Kansas. (The police officer later told me that it had, but again, the defendant was a wealthy man.) Do your best to dot your I's and cross your T's, but you are still likely doomed if your opposition is willing to pay their attorney more.

So what's the answer? *Don't go*

there. Make an offer that meets the opposing party half way, consider mediation, or give your adversary a copy of this book and then offer to work your issues out. You can do this even if you're in the middle of litigation right now. My ex-boyfriend and I did this in the middle of our paternity suit, so don't let the attorneys persuade you otherwise with their legal jargon. Ask your lawyers to provide you a bill *to date* of what you owe them (they will require you to pay them immediately for their services). After you come to an agreement with the opposing party, ask the attorneys to prepare and file a Journal Entry of your agreed resolution and a Motion to Withdraw. It's as simple as that. If they put up a fuss and try to convince you otherwise, they are looking out for their own interests—and their own pocketbooks.

You should be aware that even after all of the hard work that goes into preparing your court briefs, the judges read very little of these documents prior to a hearing; they rely on the attorneys to tell them what is in their paperwork. (It is no wonder, since our court system is inundated with so many cases that must be heard.) Judge Judy definitely has the advantage on TV because she has done her homework thoroughly. In the real world, this is not so. The judges are relying on the attorneys' opinions regarding who should win, and this is based largely on which one of them is getting paid the most money by his or her client. Since you are not an attorney and are not privy to informing the judge how *you* feel, you are doomed from the start.

The opposing attorneys already know all the tricks of their trade, so you are immediately at a disadvantage. Our Constitution guarantees individuals the right to have a lawyer appointed to represent them in a criminal matter if they can't afford one. As a result of our case, I believe that if a person has this right in a criminal case, he or she should have the same right in a civil case, especially if the other side seems determined to run you out of funds. I talked with a member of the faculty at the President's College School of Law in Wichita, and he told me the United States Supreme Court had not yet embraced this concept. I am hoping that, if our appeal reaches that far, they will consider appointed legal representation in civil cases with stipulations.

What about all the silly lawsuits that are brought to court and actually result in victory? We have heard about many of these through the news media, and it has made most of us feel paranoid. For example, in May, 2000 I went to the zoo with my son's kindergarten class. The day was bright and warm; and while all the children were lining up to enter, I took out some suntan lotion and rubbed it on my son's arms and face. A little girl in the class asked sweetly if she could have some, too. I was about to squirt some into my hand for her when the teacher shouted: "STOP! You CANNOT put that suntan lotion on her!" Of course, I froze. In a calmer tone, she explained that I could be liable for such an act and that school officials had instructed teachers to warn parents in such instances. I can't help but wonder, as many of us do, where our society is headed. . . .

Chapter Seven:
Watch Those
Innuendoes

Many lawyers, especially those who have been practicing awhile, are very good at trying to confuse you and the court in any manner they can. During a hearing, they may purposely try to confuse the chain of events in your matter. I have seen them "pick and choose" statements from depositions that support their arguments, taking them out of context from the documents from which they are extracted. While clients and witnesses are sworn to tell the truth before the judge and jury, <u>attorneys are</u> permitted to lie, if necessary, to win their client's case. It is in your best interests to object when these incidents occur so that there will be a public record of your objection noted by the court reporter in her transcript (take notes after your hearing as well, in case you have made key statements which turn up missing later on.)

My husband was appalled to hear three opposing attorneys stand up and lie to the judges during my oral arguments before the Kansas Court of Appeals in April, 2003. *A possible solution is to have the attorneys themselves be sworn in before they make their arguments!* I was also stunned when I realized from the judge's questions that they had read very little of the court record on appeal. I found out later that clerks are given this task. In my desperate effort to reveal the truth and obtain justice, I pleaded with them to be sure and read *all* of the documents in our Record on Appeal. There were twelve volumes, and they could have taken up to two years to render a decision. However, after fewer than ten weeks, they affirmed the district court's decision to dismiss, ignoring all the evidence presented, much of which was clear and convincing.

There are other innuendoes to watch for, especially during a deposition. If your case is such that you must conduct your own, this will be quite stressful for most people as it was for me. Depositions are also quite expensive, averaging $500 each for the ones I had conducted. I tried contacting several court reporting firms to let me sit in and watch an attorney conduct one, but it was not allowed. My stress level was at an all-time high trying to figure out how to depose people; however, I felt encouraged to try when I met Erin Brockovich in Oklahoma City just before the defense attorneys were going to take my deposition. (She had already known of my case from an email I had sent her and had promised to call me in a day or two—but never did. I wondered if the defendants had influenced her firm as well or if their attorneys realized that assisting in our case might result in the obvious: fewer lawsuits, faster justice and less money for attorneys. . . .)

At any rate, the feeling of hope spurred me on to conduct nine depositions in my lawsuit. (This is another reason to try to work your issues out since my health suffered throughout.) Still, on October 15, 2001, after staying up all night to prepare a court brief and conducting two depositions the next morning, I collapsed from an anxiety attack on the way to the courthouse and had to remain in bed for two days afterward.

Should you find yourself in the position of having to take depositions, it is best to have the opposing attorney schedule your deposition first; then you can take notes and learn how to proceed with deposing your own witnesses. Of course, they will find numerous reasons to object during your depositions, but just continue on with your questions even while they try to confuse you and other witnesses. From this experience, I learned that the pat answer to something one really knows but doesn't want to reveal is: "I don't recall." Why? Because if you should happen to remember it later while testifying (i.e., they catch you in a lie), you have answered safely and not perjured yourself by saying yes (or no) to a question that was asked at the time you were deposed. In this way, you can't be later found guilty of perjury. Most of the defendants I deposed seemed to be well-versed by their lawyers on this fact as well as how to hem-and-haw without giving any real answer.

If my ghastly experiences can help remind you of the need for caution, then something good may come from this situation after all. It is in your best interests to pay close and exacting attention to any legal document you are asked to sign, especially the fine print of settlement agreements. Closely read everything that is presented by the opposing attorney to the court. You say you don't understand all the "wherefore," "herein," and "heretofore" jargon? Few of us do; I almost believe that this is the primary reason lawyers phrase their laws and legal papers in such contorted and mystifying style. Even still, you need to make a concerned effort to *understand* what these documents say before you prepare your response. Remember to call your state's legal services and consult with an attorney for any general questions, especially prior to a hearing. You don't have to sign any documents you don't agree with, even those prepared by the opposing attorney after a ruling by the judge at a hearing.

Keep in mind that *if the attorneys can get something by you, they will.* As my mother always said, "There's a sucker born every minute and two to take him." But you don't have to be a sucker in the legal arena if you acquire the knowledge you need beforehand. One attorney in our suit filed a motion; and rather than requesting the motion be granted in closing, his paperwork asked for dismissal! If I hadn't noticed this and brought it up at the hearing, the judge could have dismissed my claims against his client right then and there. As it was, the judge "assumed" that counsel had made an error in the preparation of his paperwork and kindly overlooked it for him.

In other words, I cannot stress energetically enough: *carefully read EVERYTHING an attorney prepares or asks you to sign. Even more, do your best to try to understand what you've read before you respond.*

Justice

Chapter Eight:
Be Wary Of
Retainer Fees

I have only one suggestion in regard to retainer fees requested by an attorney up front. Don't agree to pay a retainer fee without a written agreement from *him* that he will refund the unused portion. You can add this to the contract you sign with him to represent you. In most other forms of business, do you pay for a service before it is rendered? Not usually—but even if you did, you would hardly do so without some assurance of a refund if not satisfied.

To illustrate: I knew of a couple who were about to split up and decided to divorce. Since it was an amicable agreement, they sought the advice of an attorney who had been a family friend for 20 years. He told them to write down all their assets and decide between them who would get what. They dutifully completed their list and dropped it off at his office. He assured them that if either one of them could get a doctor's note outlining their debilitating stress, why, the whole shebang would be over in two weeks! The couple paid his $800 fee, then waited for the paperwork to go through— and waited still more. It never did. They repeatedly called this attorney for weeks; but he never even returned their phone calls, let alone do any work for them. I couldn't help feeling that the attorney was well aware that they had assets worth fighting over and that, if he did nothing, the matter would drag out and cause them to fight while he made more money in fees. After six months, the couple got back together and called the attorney's office for a refund. Although he had never done anything to earn the $800, he refused to refund a cent of their money.

In fact, my mother had also hired the same individual in regard to a minor car accident she'd had. But she became extremely ill and was hospitalized, struggling for life, when he called her house to say she had been offered a $2800 settlement in the matter. I tearfully told him she was near death; and before he drew another breath, the attorney streaked over to the hospital to get her signature. And the outcome? Six months later, when she had recovered, I asked what she had done with the settlement check. Her eyes widened: "What check?" The attorney had kept her money! I was livid as I drove my mother to collect what he had "forgotten" to give her (minus his 40%, of course). How many other elderly people do you suppose are being duped by unethical lawyers?

From my experiences, I have

learned that if an attorney agrees to accept your case, he will do so according to one of three methods: an hourly rate, a contingency basis (usually 30-40% of your winnings), or a flat fee. It is wise to sign a contract in regard to any method that you agree upon. Most attorneys will utilize the hourly rate of payment since this assures them they will get paid whether you win or not. If you agree to this method, it is also an incentive to keep your case alive and drag it out so the attorney makes more money. In my opinion, it is wiser to choose a contingency basis, and an attorney may agree to accept on this basis if you don't have much money and he determines that your case is very strong. This is the route we took in our negligence/fraud lawsuit; however, if the opposing party is paying his attorney more money, you are very likely to lose anyway. The best way to hire an attorney is on a flat fee basis for the services he will perform. Unfortunately, most lawyers will not agree to a flat fee arrangement unless it is for a relatively simple task (e.g., drawing up a will, handling a traffic ticket, etc.)

You may get lucky and find an attorney who will agree to "ghost" your case, that is, to assist you with advice and the preparation of your court briefs but not actually represent you. During my negligence/fraud lawsuit, I was elated to find such an individual early on, an actual "honest" attorney. At a meeting in his office two months after I had filed the suit, he advised me to contact the president of our local HBA and obtain some information for the case. I faxed a letter and early the next morning received a call from the HBA president. He nastily announced that there was no information to give me in this regard. I mentioned that my attorney had asked me to get it from him, to which he bellowed: "*WHO'S* YOUR ATTORNEY??!!" I told him that I wasn't going to give him the name of my attorney after everything that had happened, and he shot back: "Well, when you file it, we'll know who it is!" Unfortunately, although I tried repeatedly to contact this attorney, I never heard from him again.

In any event, be cautious. Don't be so trusting and eager to plunk down your hard-earned money. If a lawyer will not agree in writing to refund the unused portion of any money you give him up front, quickly seek another one who will.

Justice

Chapter Nine:
The Side With
The Most
Money
(To Pay Their
Attorney) Wins

As I look back through these pages at the several illustrations of this concept I've put before you, I notice two in particular. First, in the paternity suit with my long-ago boyfriend, my attorney admitted to me that the other lawyer was being paid more. Second, in my flooding fiasco, the defendants had big bucks and knew that we had so little; indeed, even the attorney we later fired commented that we couldn't expect to win because *they* had big money and power and we didn't. The only way they could have known this was to converse with each other about it. The idea of "justice for *all*" in America is noble and highly esteemed, but does it actually exist?

I was greatly encouraged by the movie Erin Brockovich. Still, could Masry & Vititoe have won their case if their firm had not partnered with another attorney who had lavish funds and a great deal of clout? For that matter, does anyone really believe that O.J. Simpson was innocent? We all know that he had big bucks to spend, for sure, and "money talks." This is a question worth pondering.

It was evident in our lawsuit that the matter kept dragging out because the attorneys wanted to make more money; and even though we should have rightfully won, their clients had paid big dollars so they had to win (otherwise, they could have faced malpractice claims by their clients). All in all, it appears pretty obvious that money does, in fact, buy justice: actually what it buys is *injustice.*

So *is there justice*? I have had trouble finding it. I was flabbergasted when our previous attorney explained: "I know, I know what your problem is . . . you think that just because there's a justice system, there's justice. Well, I'm here to tell you, there's not. You think all these guys aren't going to get up there and lie about everything they told you? I guarantee you they will. I've only worked one case in my entire career (20 years) where everyone told the truth." Later on, two other attorneys commented to me wholeheartedly that they agreed: there is no justice in America today. One of them even told me that he would agree with this statement "ten thousand percent."

So where does that leave the Pledge of Allegiance? As children, we recited this daily in school, having it drilled into our heads as a necessary and worthy part of our life's education. We, along with our children today, repeat this pledge as a component of our belief in the goodness of our system of government. But after what we have experienced, a friend of mine recently confided that he could no longer repeat the last line: ". . . and justice for *all*." The reality is that *apparent* justice exists primarily for those who have the funds to buy victory. So to be less hypocritical, should we revise the Pledge of Allegiance? No. Instead, let us each work to restore the true justice our forefathers intended.

Chapter Ten:
If At All Possible, Don't Go There

"Discourage litigation. Persuade your neighbors to compromise whenever you can. Point out to them the nominal winner is often a real loser in fees, expenses and waste of time."

Abraham Lincoln

If these words were true in the simpler times of a century and a half ago, only think of their relevance in today's increasingly litigious society. No doubt Abraham

Lincoln would be appalled to see what we've become. Respected by many as our greatest president, he is revered because he was *for the people*. He was a self-taught lawyer and known to history as "Honest Abe." How many present-day attorneys would fit that description? As for me as well as countless others, he has been a mentor and my greatest inspiration.

In all honesty, after reading this book, do you still feel like filing a lawsuit against someone? Are you ready to lose your money and suffer the stress that accompanies such an ordeal? Is it really worth it?

Certainly I never imagined what the prolonged stress of my three-year ordeal could do to my health. Not to be overly dramatic, I'll just mention a life focused on and swimming in a sea of negativity, depression, suicidal thoughts, anxiety attacks, paranoia, stress headaches, chest pains, contact dermatitis, eye ulcers and recurring viral infections, neurodermatitis, basil cell carcinoma re-quiring Mohs surgery, osteoarthritis, neck and back pain severe enough to rob me of sleep. I've mentioned a near divorce from the stress, my children distraught over the lack of money, and the irrevers-ible scars inflicted on my son from being falsely charged—all of these situations stemming from the lawsuit. I have been boycotted in the areas of construction and real estate in my town to the point that the three houses I had built (in four years) would not sell for months. Real-tors would not even show my homes to prospective buyers for fear of being black-listed in the industry. Not even trying to understand my situation, friends I had known for 25 years stopped associating with me, and even the few I had hoped would testify in my behalf would ignore me when I ran into them on the street. And after enduring all this, we have not even won the case. It is ironic to see frivo-lous lawsuits won and non-frivolous law-suits dismissed.

Again, would it not be better to avoid litigation—to try to work out the problems rather than making some attorney richer? If the money you are seeking or the issues involved are minor, you are better off to chalk it up to lessons learned and move on. Weigh the realities of emotional and physical pain and a probable loss of the case against the almost knee-jerk impulse our society encourages: "Sue the bum(s)!" Such action is an option, of course; but count the cost to your life and well-being before you feed some fat cat's wallet.

If my writing this book keeps at least one person from filing an unnecessary lawsuit against someone else, if it helps him or her decide to avoid all that pain and disruption, I won't consider my efforts to have been in vain. Consider the attorney who told me in front of witnesses in June 2001 that "they're just going to keep 'beating you up' until they wear you down." I believe most people in a civilized culture would find it unacceptable to purposefully inflict pain on others, especially to win a lawsuit. Police were severely thrashed for physically beating up Rodney King who appeared to be a criminal. Shouldn't it be even more unacceptable, then, to emotionally beat up a person who is innocent? If intentional emotional distress is against the law, why is this an accepted practice in our legal system to win lawsuits? We should no longer tolerate such conduct from a profession we traditionally esteem so highly. In the words of my pastor: "God expects *everyone* to obey the laws of the land."

Under the Constitution, the Sixth Amendment guarantees our right to legal representation in a criminal matter. We are appointed an attorney according to certain guidelines that must be met. It is my belief that this right should extend to persons in a civil matter as well, with stipulations, especially if the opposing party runs you out of money. Furthermore, the right to be appointed an attorney in a civil matter should be decided by the people rather than by lawyers or judges in the court system; this would be a step in ensuring that government "of the people, by the people and for the people" will not perish from the earth.

Still, if you absolutely must go there, keep these ten issues in mind. If you now have a better idea of the negative realities involved with automatically trusting our legal system, these ten warnings can help you prepare mentally for what is ahead. Hopefully, they will keep unethical attorneys from taking advantage of you.

Conclusion/
Recommendations

I'll get down off of my soap box now. In general, and if at all possible, avoid getting into a lawsuit. And the next time you hear that someone was found guilty, not guilty, or the charges were dismissed, don't automatically assume that he or she was or that justice prevailed. Ask yourself instead: which side had the most money to pay their attorney? I would challenge those of you involved in past litigation or going through a lawsuit at the present time—dare to compare your attorney bills! It would be interesting to know the percentage of cases won by the side who actually paid their attorney less. Our government needs to take steps to eliminate money from the equation and ensure justice is available to all. And if the government won't, we need to make this a personal decision to do our small part to reverse such trends in our country.

Someone commented to me once that there is no longer a middle class in America. There is the upper class (the rich, who don't have to worry), and the lower class (the poor and the struggling, those who live from paycheck to paycheck). While television shows like "Lifestyles of the Rich and Famous" detail the surreal, almost obscene trappings of wealth, *the majority* of our citizens are toiling away simply to make ends meet. And hasn't it reached the point where most families can only survive on two paychecks? If all men are created equal under the law, then even the poor and the struggling, those living from paycheck to paycheck, should be able to win a lawsuit if they have a good case. Clearly, the way the profession works needs a major overhaul.

In regard to our litigation, I have even begun to see a small flicker of light at the end of the tunnel of justice. In 2002, a colleague suggested that I meet a woman who was encountering very similar frustrations with the legal system. She was a doctor's wife who had been trying for several years to obtain a public school education for her autistic son. But after finally winning her suit, she had incurred $75,000 in attorney fees for her son's right to a "free" education. We met several times, and one day she called to tell me that her legal battle was finally over and thanked me for how much I had helped her. She mentioned that she had confronted her counsel who were afraid that she was going to sue them for malpractice (how would that look, she said— a doctor's wife suing a lawyer?) She was given a $35,000 settlement, and her lawyers dropped the $75,000 in attorney fees she was going to have to pay.

It was during this time that a lawyer told me that the district court could have ordered us into mediation at any time in our lawsuit. But why didn't they? I'm guessing it's because they were still trying to convince us it was a "nothing" case. And if it was, why were so many insurance companies refusing to insure small builders in early 2003? I consulted about 50 of them to try to get insurance; and when I finally got some, the policy had a "new" exclusion: there was to be no coverage for property damage or bodily injury arising from a failure to render professional engineering services (like leaving a drainage easement off of a plat). At the same time, several states, including Kansas, passed legislation which now makes it extremely difficult to try to sue a builder or developer for any wrongdoing on his or her part during construction. It seems that insurance is being made to protect all but those who need it. . . .

I have concluded that one possible way to ensure justice is to computerize all the evidence in a case. With so many other parts of our world being handled efficiently and fairly by computers, wouldn't the legal system benefit from this type of solution? Computerization could also assist judges and jurors in rendering an accurate decision in cases; that is, the claims and any applicable statute and case law could be input into a database along with all the available evidence provided by the plaintiff and defendant. The machinery could ascertain two things: Does the plaintiff's evidence meet the criteria needed to support a conviction of the defendant? Does the defendant's evidence meet the criteria needed to support an acquittal? If the evidence is so strong that a conviction is likely (say, 75% or better), then the matter is not left up to the attorneys hoping to further prolong the case, drain your pocketbook, and cause you unneeded stress.

Let's say, for example, you have a claim against someone for breach of contract. You contact an attorney and give him all your evidence (a copy of the contract, witnesses and their comments, affidavits, etc.). Your lawyer inputs your information into the database while the defense attorney does the same with the evidence against your claim presented by the defendant. The program would disregard the social and economic status of both parties but would take into account all of the laws, statutes, and case law in regard to the claims involved. If a conviction is likely (as we have suggested, 75% or better), these facts are divulged to both attorneys and their clients and would be available to any judges or jurors in an impending lawsuit. Of course, the defendant would have the option of settling or dropping the suit if the numbers are not in his favor. Such a process would eliminate the human factor of attorneys who seek to intimidate and stress their clients and needlessly prolong their issues. Let the computer make the decision to go forward based on the merits of the case alone, regardless of a person's income, their past, and any weaknesses an attorney might be able to draw out and exploit. If the case is strongly in the plaintiff's favor and the defendant refuses to settle, then at least the plaintiff goes forward with less anxiety and more confidence that the outcome is likely to be a win on his side.

Without being presumptuous, I'll tentatively call this technique the "Farr Factor," named for my father who was a fighter pilot killed in Viet Nam. (I believe we all need to capture that fighting spirit to change the misconduct in the legal profession!) During this process, the judge and jury would still make the ultimate decision if the matter goes to trial. This is in keeping with our constitutional right to a trial—and by a jury—if we so choose. Quite possibly such a method has already been developed by the legal profession because Catherine Crier seems to imply something to this effect in her book *The Case Against Lawyers*. Does it exist, and . . . hmmm . . . are they keeping it from us?

As I mentioned earlier during my appeal, I had sent my editorial letter to 100 major newspapers in every city in the United States and to President Bush in March, 2002. Not receiving any response, I sent a follow-up letter in July, 2002. Two months later, I got a letter from the Justice Department, indicating that my letter had been referred to them. They graciously apologized for not contacting me sooner, but this was all their letter said. In early November I decided to call the Justice Department outright to learn if they had plans to respond.

I was impressed that an actual human voice answered the phone! In speaking with the woman in Washington, I asked politely if they were going to send me a letter in response to my concerns. She admitted that the letter I already received *was* their answer. Since I observed that it didn't really say anything, she explained that they don't address personal issues. When I insisted further that "it's what lawyers are doing to lots of people, not just me. Doesn't anyone *care?*" Her fascinating reply is a classic: the justice department receives a great many letters, and they are naturally concerned; but "they don't really do anything." Since I could think of nothing else to say at that point, I asked, "What did you say your name was?" She told me she wasn't allowed to give out her name.

I would have left it there except that two weeks later, I received a manila envelope with the return address "The White House." Inside was a very impressive letter suitable for framing which thanked me for my concern about "corporate fraud." It was signed by President George W. Bush. I decided to send him a copy of my court brief and ask for such an investigation, also sending copies to the FBI and SEC. I received responses from all three; and the FBI was investigating, but they could not tell me anything else.

We have needed improvements in our legal system for years, but for too long our congressmen—most of them attorneys—have been ordering things to benefit their colleagues rather than the average American. We might conclude that they would be against such changes because members of the legal profession would no longer be able to drag out cases and make additional money off of the prolonged pain and suffering they can cause us. Many people believe that because a court ruled in a certain way, it was the truth in a matter. But from my experiences, I have learned that their decisions were largely based on money rather than truth. There are a lot of innocent people in jail; maybe now we know why.

I am convinced that there is only one way to solve the lawyer problem: force them to be more honest. A significant indication that the situation is out of hand is the number of ridiculous lawsuits being filed. Even more, many people live in fear of being sued, yet we can eliminate this anxiety by refusing to be a part of it, by working out our issues instead of charging into lawsuits. I believe that the Golden Rule should apply—that if you treat people right and make an effort to work with them in a dispute, they will not be inclined to sue you—and vice versa. And it is amazing how the simple words "I'm sorry" can change the emotions and intent of both parties involved. We need to stop making attorneys richer and demand that our government incorporate changes to ensure actual justice in our so-called justice system.

Do people who bring such frivolous lawsuits have money to begin with and the desire to indulge in such a fight? My guess is that many of them are struggling, so desperate for cash (convinced by an attorney—on a contingency basis, of course) that they're willing to play the victim to obtain it. Even more troubling are these attorneys, aware that most people have confidence in everything they say, who are talking these individuals into filing such suits.

This appears to be a huge problem when it comes to class action suits. A regional manager for an insurance company confided this story to me in May 2003. He said it all started when a house burned down in a California development, apparently due to faulty wiring. Lawyers then knocked on the doors of homeowners in the same development and persuaded them to join a class-action suit against the same builder/developer who happened to have "deep pockets." He went on to explain that it had gotten so bad that lawyers were buying up condos just to inspect them, hoping to find something wrong so they could get people to file class-action suits. In his words: "Now the legislature is trying to figure out what to do about the lawyer problem."

In closing, if you are in any way doubtful as to whether the events of our litigation took place, our court case is a matter of public record. Anyone can review our court files at the Sedgwick County courthouse in Wichita, Kansas (Case No. 01 C 0771 and 03 CV 1655) or the Kansas Court of Appeals in Topeka (Case No. 02-88617-A). There are over twelve volumes of evidence to look through, and I am hoping by the time you read this, they are not all destroyed or replaced with some other case. I imagine the media would be out there saying that there is no evidence so it can't be true, dissecting my life and insisting I'm a whacko; I can see it all coming. So I hope you will take me at my word.

When it comes to litigation, make it a personal decision and don't go there. They're playing games with your life and your money, and they don't care if you get hurt. I say: *"Game over."*

About
The Author

Joan Farr received her Bachelor's and Master's degrees in Administration of Justice from Wichita State University in 1977 and 1981 respectively. She served on the Wichita Police Department as a traffic investigator from 1982-1984. While employed as a purchasing agent at the Boeing Company in Wichita, she assisted in the interior construction of Air Force One from 1986-1990. She was born in Weisbaden, Germany, the daughter of a court reporter and an Air Force pilot killed in Viet Nam. She was the first woman builder to join the Wichita Area Builders' Association in 1999. Joan is currently a member of the National Association of Home Builders and the NAHB Women's Council. She has been listed as an Honored Professional in the National Register's Who's Who in Executives and Professionals, and is a 2001 Honoree of the International Who's Who of Professional and Business Women.

Joan is a self-taught lawyer, architect and homebuilder as well as an accomplished artist and interior designer. She currently designs, builds and decorates spec homes in the Wichita area. In 2003, she began a non-profit organization called the Association for Honest Attorneys (A.H.A!), dedicated to discouraging litigation, preserving justice, and improving the legal system in America. Joan lives in Sedgwick County, Kansas, with her husband, Mark, and four sons. You can visit the association's web site at www.assocforhonestattys.com